MAPPING IRELAND
FROM KINGDOMS TO COUNTIES

D0552199

SEÁN CONNORS

MERCIER PRESS

MERCIER PRESS
5 French Church Street, Cork
16 Hume Street, Dublin 2

Trade enquiries to COLUMBA MERCIER DISTRIBUTION,
55a Spruce Avenue, Stillorgan Industrial Park, Blackrock, Dublin

© Seán Connors 2001

ISBN 1 85635 355 9

10 9 8 7 6 5 4 3 2 1

DEDICATION
*To the memory of my father Edmund Connors
and
to Vanessa for her patience*

My grateful thanks to everyone who assisted me in producing this collection, in particular; Gerard Enwright and Anike Tyrrell of The Waterford County Enterprise Board, The Deputy Chief Herald Fergus Gillespie, Office of the Chief Herald, Dublin, Michael McNicholas, Enterprise Ireland, New York and the many others who were kind enough to provide local information that would otherwise have been very difficult to find. A special mention to Tracey Barlow for her exceptional computer skills.

Printed in Ireland by Colour Books Ltd.

MAPPING IRELAND
FROM KINGDOMS TO COUNTIES

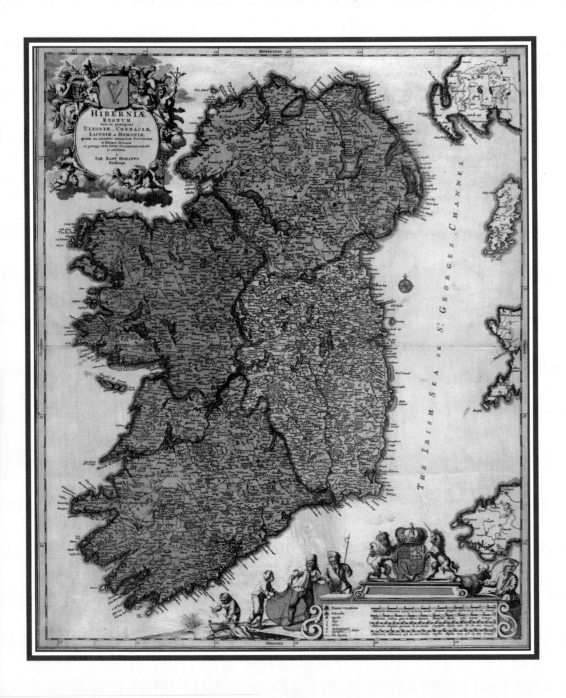

CONTENTS

THE IRISH DIASPORA

Precariously perched on Europe's westernmost extremities in the turbulent Atlantic Ocean Ireland, in global terms, is a tiny almost insignificant island. Measuring approximately 300 miles at its longest and 200 miles at its widest the impact of this small country on so much of the world is unparalleled.

In the Middle Ages Ireland was known as one of the leading centres of learning and culture in all of Europe earning the name – 'The Island of Saints and Scholars'. It was not however until the advent of deportation and emigration that the huge Irish global presence began to be felt. Beginning as a slow trickle in the early 1700s emigration rose to a deluge during the great potato blight of the 1840s. These few years were among the darkest in Ireland's history with over two million people fleeing their homes or dying from starvation or disease.

Those lucky enough to make a new life elsewhere brought with them the wonderful richness of their cultural heritage. The music and dance, and the strong oral traditions, they inherited from their forebears were all preserved and passed on to later generations. Thanks to these traditions tens of millions of their descendants worldwide still maintain a huge emotional attachment to Ireland. This is the Irish Diaspora – one large family separated by time and distance but all sharing a common heritage and, of course, homeplace – that tiny insignificant island on the western edge of Europe – Ireland.

This collection of county maps has been created as a celebration of the Irish Diaspora. By combining a 300-year-old original document with the most modern computer and printing technology this is the first fully digitised complete and matching collection of Ireland and her counties ever created. This book allows Irish people worldwide to own a unique view of their native land and to display their Irishness with pride and dignity. Above all these images promote a sense of belonging. They are what unite us all – they are home.

A Short History of the Mapping of Ireland

In the second century AD the information stored in the great library of Alexandria and the first hand accounts of the seafarers who passed through this great Egyptian port allowed Claudius Ptolemy to list the positions of sixty features of Ireland. Sited mostly on the east coast they included rivers, headlands, towns and islands. It was not however until around 1200AD that Ireland began to appear in the more elaborate *mappae mundi* of mediaeval Europe. Increased trade with Italy earned it a place on more accurate sea charts from around 1300AD.

The earliest known printed map of Ireland was produced in Italy in 1528. This was followed by a series of mostly crude maps printed in Rome and Venice around the 1560s.

By the end of the 1500s the Tudor conquest of Ireland had extended British rule beyond the Pale and across the rest of the country. The mapping of Ireland took a more sinister twist when British cartographers, following in the wake of their conquering armies, began drawing regional maps of territories declared forfeit to the crown and British planters. The 1600s saw a steadily increasing number of such land acquisitions always preceded by fiercely fought and bloody campaigns.

The culmination of these bloody land acquisitions were the staggeringly brutal campaigns of Oliver Cromwell in the 1650s. Cromwell set out once and for all to quell the Irish spirit of revolt. Fuelled by a pathological hatred for Roman Catholicism, and a hatred for Irish people in general, he seized large tracts of the country and banished what remained of the ruling classes to the barren lands of the west with the infamous words 'to hell or to Connacht'.

In the aftermath of these campaigns the physician–general of the British army in Ireland, William Petty, was charged with recording, in detail, all lands forfeit by the Irish. Equipped with the most modern instruments and an army of over 1,000 surveyors and clerks Petty produced the definitive and incredibly thorough 'Down Survey' – so called because all measurements taken in the field were immediately written down on site for greater accuracy. His was the first map to depict Ireland's true shape and was so accurate that it was extensively used by other cartographers for many years to come. It remains visually correct to the present day.

It is this map which has now formed the basis for the earliest possible complete and matching set of maps of the counties of Ireland ever produced.

The Evolution of the Counties of Ireland

The organisation of modern Ireland into its thirty-two county components is such an accepted fact that for almost all of us it warrants no consideration whatsoever. Yet, of all the legacies we inherit from our troubled past, the county system is one of the most important and least appreciated. Even a cursory investigation of the evolution of the county system reveals, to a certain degree, the foundation of the general history of Ireland itself. For the county system was a direct result of the 'shiring' of Ireland – the process by which the territories of Ireland were eventually brought under English administration. This process was slow and intermittent, taking many centuries between the reign of King John (1199–1216) – some say as early as that of Henry II (1154–89) – until well into the seventeenth century.

Ireland at that time was made up of five kingdoms. Each was ruled by a king (*rí*) and one of these would be named, by general agreement, *ardrí* or high king. Although the territories appear to have been well-defined the inhabitants were tribal and warlike. There was constant unrest between provincial kings which led in 1167 to Dermot Mac Murrough of Leinster losing his throne and going into exile from Ireland. Mac Murrough sought help from the English king, Henry II who allowed him to enlist the aid of Richard FitzGilbert de Clare, Earl of Pembroke in Wales, known to all as Strongbow. By 1169, with Strongbow's assistance, he had reclaimed the throne of Leinster.

In 1171 Henry and his army landed at Waterford. He was largely unopposed due to the supposed existence of a papal letter *Laudabiliter* issued by Adrian IV (the only English pope) in 1155 which gave Ireland to Henry to reform. Adrian's successor, Pope Alexander III did issue three letters; one to Irish Church leaders reproving them for the state of the Irish people; one to the Irish kings and princes praising them for willingly submitting to Henry and one to Henry himself charging him with the task of reforming Irish customs.

This then was the Ireland of the Anglo-Norman invasions: wild, ancient kingdoms made up of clan territories which were ruled by might rather than central government or settled constitution.

The first division of Ireland into counties was effected just after the Anglo-Norman invasions. The earliest grants of land had been made by Henry II in the form of palatine counties with some additional divisions created by his son King John. Henry granted all of Ireland to his followers so that, even though they possessed less than one-third of the land, they owned all in title, leaving nothing for the native population. Of the original grants by Henry at least three were palatinates: Leinster to Strongbow, Meath to De Lacy and Ulster to De Courcy. By the time of John's death in 1216 there were twelve shires in Munster and Leinster: Dublin, Kildare, Meath, Urial (Louth), Catherlogh (Carlow), Kilkenny, Wexford, Waterford, Cork, Limerick, Kerry and Tipperary. These were identifiable geographical areas but were not yet counties in the modern sense as administration of any kind did not begin until many years after John's death.

To follow the process of county development it is important to understand the difference between the Palatine and ordinary county.

The institution of counties in England is pre-Norman with the title and office of count having been derived from the court of Charlemagne. The creation of a count involved a delegation of royal authority for legal and administrative purposes. The county had two courts: king's court for criminal cases and the earl's court for civil cases. In the ordinary county the sheriffs and officers were appointed directly by the crown.

In the palatine county the earl was lord of all the lands in his shire except Church land and his authority was equal to the king's in an ordinary county. Such a massive delegation of power only occurred where a sovereign could not establish effective administration throughout his realm. Henry, in effect, handed Ireland over to Strongbow and his followers with powers equivalent to those of the crown. The exceptions being Church land and some coastal towns and areas that were reserved for the sovereign. Where the crown did appoint sheriffs to the palatinate their authority extended only to the lands of the Church and they were known as Sheriffs of the County of the Cross. There must have been at least as many counties of the cross as there were palatinates but the reabsorption of the palatinates into crown control, mainly through marriage or the passing of new laws (as in the case of Henry VIII and Meath) resulted in their virtual extinction by the end of that king's reign in 1547. The only exception was Tipperary which survived until after the Restoration in 1660.

The English system of territory division was outlined in a paper by Bishop Reeves (1815–92) entitled 'The Townland Distribution of Ireland'. In it he states *'The civil distribution of Ireland, in the descending scale, is into provinces, counties, baronies, parishes and townslands'*. He gives the following brief description of each: *'The provinces, subject to one suppression and some interchange of adjacent territories, represent a very ancient native partition which, in the twelfth century was adopted for ecclesiastical purposes. The counties and baronies, though principally based on groupings of native lordships, are of Anglo-Norman origin, and range, in the date of their creation from the reign of King John to that of James I. (From pre 1216– 1620s.) The parochial division is entirely borrowed from the Church, under which it matured probably about the middle of the twelfth century; while the townslands, the infima species, may reasonably be considered, at least in part, the earliest allotment in scale'.*

The parishes and townslands have little or nothing to do with the development of the county system but the baronies deserve some consideration in their own right.

The barony was the key territorial division within the county. There seems little doubt that the early baronies were formed on the submission of Irish chieftains and therefore represented most closely the ancient tribal territories. (This would explain why modern Irish counties have such irregular and seemingly pointless shapes. Ancient clan territories would have been defined mainly by geographical features such as mountains, rivers, valleys or woods, etc. While demarcation of this kind would have made perfect sense to the people on the ground it lost meaning when drawn on a map.) The early baronies however were continually sub-divided until, by the time of the census of 1901, there were some 327 in the country. It is interesting that the name 'barony' as a division of a county seems to have had no such meaning in the territorial classification of Great Britain. The Irish barony came into existence when the kingdom of Meath was granted to the elder De Lacy who portioned it out to his lesser barons to be held under him by feudal service. These estates took the name of baronies and gradually spread to similar sub-divisions of other counties.

The provinces had no official administrative function for the early Anglo-Normans and would most probably have disappeared were they not of such importance to the early Church. Christianity could only spread with the permission of the provincial kings and consequently provincial boundaries were respected land divisions for early missionaries. If Meath and Westmeath were regarded as one province, Mide, as it was known, it and the other four provinces seem to present a very accurate picture of the ancient kingdoms of Ireland.

Some changes which occurred to the provinces during the shiring process were:

- Ulster originally included Louth but not Cavan.

- Munster originally included the territory of Ely (O'Carroll country) which later formed two baronies in King's County (Offaly) now part of Leinster.

- Connacht included Cavan and a part of Longford while during the sixteenth century Clare, known as the Earldom of Thomond, interchanged between Connacht and Munster before finally remaining part of the southern province.

- Meath appears to have been almost identical to the modern counties of Meath and Westmeath although it may have included part of Longford.

- Leinster was made up of its modern counties, without Louth, Meath, Westmeath and the Ely O'Carroll territory mentioned above.

For a full century after John's death his twelve shires continued to represent the full extent of English rule until the invasion of Edward the Bruce in 1315. The wars of the Bruces delivered a blow to the English colony from which it did not recover for almost two hundred years. The control of the crown diminished during this time until, by the 1500s, its full extent was the Pale – as described in the State Papers of Henry VIII: '*Also the English Pale doth stretch and extend from the town of Dundalk to the town of Derver, to the town of Ardee, always on the left side leaving the march* (border) *on the right side, and so to the town of Sydan, to the town of Kenlys* (Kells), *to the town of Dangle* (Dangan), *to Kilcock, to the town of Clane, to the town of Naas, to the bridge of Cucullyn* (Kilcullen), *to the town of Ballymore* (Ballymore-Eustace), *and so backward to the town of Ramore* (Rathmore), *and to the town of Rathcoole, to the town of Tallaght, to the town of Dalkey, leaving always the march on the right hand from the said Dundalk following the said course to the said town of Dalkey'*.

There is no indication that any new counties were created in the three hundred years between the time of King John and that of the Tudors but records are sparse. This is due to the wanton destruction of most of the early records of the Kingdom of Ireland during the reigns of Edward I (known as Longshanks) (1272–1307) and his immediate successor Edward II (1307–27). Records concerning the appointment of sheriffs did survive however and they show that the only new appointment was upon the sub-division of Connacht into the territories of Connacht and Roscommon.

During most of this time the ancient tribal divisions of Ireland were still very much in use by the native Irish and were even recognised right up to the middle of the sixteenth century. In the State Papers of Henry VIII it was written that if the king desired to reform his lands in Ireland '*it is necessary to show him the estate of all the noble folk of the same, as well of the king's subjects and English rebels, as of the Irish enemies. And first of all to make his grace understand that there may be more than 60 countries, called regions in Ireland, inhabited with the king's Irish enemies ... where reigneth more than 60 chief captains ... that liveth only by the sword and obeyeth to no other temporal persons, but only to himself that is strong.'* Long into the imposition of the county system the native Irish still obeyed their own rules as noted by Sir John Davies ... *'during the reign of Philip and Mary (circa 1557) ... the Provinces of Connaught and Ulster and a good part of Leinster were not reduced to shire ground ... and though Munster was anciently divided into counties, the people were so degenerate as no justice durst execute his commission among them'.*

With such diminished authority the extension of Irish counties between the reigns of Edward II and Henry VIII (1327–1509) was virtually impossible.

In the sixteenth century the second phase of county creation began.

1534 Henry VIII decided to exert complete supremacy over Ireland and passed a law making himself King of Ireland.

1542 He reclaimed Meath for the crown and divided it into Meath and Westmeath. This not only made for easier administration but also ensured that it would never again be a palatinate. This was his only contribution to the formation of Ireland's counties but under him and his daughter, Elizabeth I (1558–1603), the Pale was greatly enlarged to include Leinster, Meath and Louth.

The shiring of Connacht, Ulster and part of Leinster was carried out first by the Earl of Sussex, Sir Henry Sidney and later Sir John Perrot.

1556 During the reign of Mary Tudor (Bloody Mary) a statute was passed declaring the king and queen heirs and successors to the territories of Leix, Slewmargy, Irry, Glenmarily and Offaly.

1557 These districts, home to the powerful O'Moores and O'Connors, were planted under the Vice-royalty of the Earl of Sussex. Sussex had a grand plan to divide Ireland into six parts: the five provinces with Munster divided in two. He was recalled before putting his plan into action.

1566 Sidney gave orders that a bridge be built at Athlone and a few years later another one at Ballinasloe. These were vital to improve communications and to facilitate the movement of troops to maintain British rule. With these bridges came the administrative machinery and the shiring of Sligo, Mayo, Galway and Roscommon. The territories of the O'Ferralls [O'Farrells] and the O'Reillys, known as Annaly and East Breny, were formed into Longford and Cavan.

1569 Elizabeth I passed a statute for *'turning of countries that be not yet shire ground into shire ground ... so that Her Majesty's laws may have free course throughout this whole realm of Ireland.'*

1570 Sidney begins forming the system of presidents that would govern Munster and Connacht for the next seventy years. Perrot became the first President of Munster. His records show eight counties there: five English shires; Cork, Limerick, Waterford, Kerry and Tipperary and three Irish shires; Desmond, Ormond and Thomond. Munster was a problem for Sidney and he elected to reduce its size by placing the territory of Thomond (Co. Clare), under the rule of the president of Connacht. Clare remained part of Connacht until almost the end of Elizabeth's reign when it became a separate division and was governed by the Earls of Thomond. Ormond was Tipperary less the County of the Cross of Tipperary and Desmond was a less clearly defined area between East Kerry and West Cork.

1571 The territory of Desmond was briefly elevated to the status of county before being amalgamated with Kerry by 1606.

1578 Sidney's position as Lord Deputy ended and the Desmond rebellion effectively put a stop to the shiring process. Irish rule still prevailed in the areas south-west of Dublin, the most important families being the Kavanaghs, Byrnes, O'Tooles and Mayles. These lands were bounded out into a shire and named Wicklow. This shiring was carried out by Sidney's successor Sir William Drury but the troubles in Munster and Ulster left him so little time to enforce the law that by 1590 the Irish families were once again 'Thorns in the side of the Pale'.

Wexford at this time was said still to be inhabited by the descendants of the first conquerors. Both Sidney and Drury found that here *'there were no sufficient and sure gentlemen to be sheriffs nor freeholders to make a jury for Her Majesty'* and overlooked its shiring. Their successor, Sir John Perrot, came to a similar conclusion. In a letter to Elizabeth he wrote *'The Birnes, Tooles and Kavanaghs must be reduced ... They are ready firebrands of rebellion to the O'Moores and O'Connors and, till they be brought under or extirped, Dublin, Kildare, Meath, Westmeath and the King's and Queen's counties cannot be clear either of them or of the O'Moores or O'Connors, or the incursions and spoils of the McGeoghegans, O'Molloys and other Irish borderers'.*

1583 Leitrim was shired under Perrot.

1584 Perrot succeeded to the Irish Government and the shiring process continued. He was largely responsible for dividing Ulster into counties although it was at least twenty years before the divisions were recognised. He made seven shires in Ulster; Armagh, Monaghan, Tyrone, Coleraine, Donegal, Fermanagh and Cavan. His work was interrupted by the rising of Hugh O'Neill but a few years later, after the Flight of the Earls and the Plantation of Ulster, his land divisions were finally in use.

The only counties in Ulster before Elizabeth's time were Louth, Antrim and Down. The other districts had existed prior to Edward II (1307–1327) but from then until Antrim was settled by the McDonnells of the Isles little is known of them.

1588 Perrot was recalled in disgrace and the shiring process stopped for nearly twenty years.

During this time maps and written testimony show many discrepancies in the county borders. For example in 1598 Haynes' *Description of Ireland* names five provinces with Meath containing four counties – East Meath, West Meath, Longford and Cavan. In a survey in 1602 Longford is included with Connacht while Cavan is not mentioned.

1606 The end stage of the shiring process was begun by Sir Arthur Chichester under the first Stuart king, James I. Between 1606 and 1610 the county boundaries of Ulster and Connacht were confirmed – mainly in Perrot's original arrangement. It took some years to delineate these counties but by 1619 the process was practically complete.

The shiring of Wicklow was finally completed.

Tipperary was the last of the palatine counties. It and the County of the Cross of Tipperary continued to be represented separately in the Irish House of Commons until Strafford's Government in 1634. The palatinate was created by a grant of Edward III in 1328 to James Le Botiller, Earl of Ormond and confirmed by successive monarchs to the Butler family. It was seized into the crown in 1621 by James I but its County of the Cross remained unaffected. Four years after the Restoration, Charles II granted the entire county to the first Duke of Ormond. The Butlers ruled until 1715 when Tipperary was made an ordinary county and the shiring of Ireland was finally complete.

ÉIRE / IRELAND

Ireland's name is said to derive from the Celtic *Íar or Éir* meaning 'west', suggesting that the early inhabitants were fully aware of their country's geographical position. It has been suggested that the word *Íar* may have roots in the ancient Sanskrit word *avara* meaning posterior or western. *Íar* was sometimes pronounced as 'Iver' or 'Iliver' from which evolved the names 'Iris', 'Ierna', 'Juverna', 'Iverna', 'Hibernia' and eventually, Ireland. At some time or another in the past Ireland has been known by all of these names. The oldest form of the native name is Eriu but there is conjecture that it may have derived from an even older native form 'Iberiu' or 'Iveriu'. The reason given is that in the most ancient writings, such as St Patrick's *Confession*, the Latin forms *Hiberio, Hibernia or Iberio* are used. Also, the Welsh and Breton names for Ireland are *Ywerddon, Iwerdon* and *Iverdon*. In modern Gaelic it has always been written as *Éire* which gave rise to the Anglo-Saxon name 'Iraland' (the land of Ira or Éire).

In legend, Ireland was known by three names Éire, Fódla and Bánba. These were the names of the wives of three kings of the Dé Dannan 'Mac Coll', 'Mac Kecht' and 'Mac Grena'. Another romantic name was 'Inisfáil' – 'The Island of Fál'. 'Fál' or 'Lia-Fáil' was the name of the coronation stone brought to Ireland by the Dé Dannan. Ireland was also, at one time, known as *Scotia* but this name passed to Scotland after that country was settled by 'Scots' from Ireland.

Cavan
County
1710

AN CABHÁN / CAVAN

MEANING OF COUNTY NAME:

In the Irish language *Cabhán* means a hollow or a cavity as in a field hollow. Yet in some areas it has been taken to mean just the opposite – a round dry hill. This gradual change of meaning probably occurred over a long period of time. In this case the physical appearance of the place leaves no doubt as Cavan itself stands in a large hollow.

BARONIES:

Castlerahan – Clankee – Clanmahon – Loughtee Lower – Loughtee Upper – Tullygarvey – Tullyhaw – Tullyhunco.

MOST COMMON NAMES:

McCabe – McGovern – O'Reilly – McKiernan – O'Donohoe –McAtilla (Flood) – O'Farrelly – O'Sheridan – O'Curry – O'Clery – McGowan – O'Mulready – McCoyle – McBrady – McIlduff.

Clare
County
1710

HIBERNIÆ
REGNUM
tam in principas
ULTONIÆ, CONNACIÆ,
LACENIÆ et MOMONIÆ,
quam in minores earundem Provincias
et Ditiones divisum
et prototype GUIL PETIT VICHERDARO Deducto
et exhibitum
à
IOH. BAPT. HOMANNO
Noribergæ

AN CLAR

Sheilds by permission of Chief Herald's office

An Clár / Clare

MEANING OF COUNTY NAME:

The Irish word *Clár* literally means a board or a plank and has been used in this sense wherever there may have been a plank of wood used to bridge a small river or stream. It has also been used to describe a very flat plain. Clare County appears to have been named after the village of the same name where the locals used a plank to serve as a bridge over the river Fergus.

BARONIES:

Bunratty Lower – Bunratty Upper – Burren – Clonderalaw – Corcomroe – Ibrickan – Inchiquin – Islands – Leitrim – Moyarta – Tulla Lower – Tulla Upper.

MOST COMMON NAMES:

O'Daly – O'Loughlin – O'Davoren – O'Hanrahan – O'Connor – O'Boland – O'Tyne – McCurtin – O'Hehir – O'Quinn – Crowe – Mulqueen – Brady – O'Minogue – O'Hickey – O'Slattery – O'Clohessy – McDonnell – O'Dea – McGorman – O'Mulvey – McInerney – McKeane – Lynch – O'Donnell – McMahon – O'Carmody – McNamara – Aherne – McGrath – O'Regan – McSheedy – McEnright.

Westmeath
County
1710

IARMHÍ

Sheilds by permission of Chief Herald's office

An Íarmhí / Westmeath

MEANING OF COUNTY NAME:

Íar in the Irish language means 'west'. Westmeath and Meath was originally one territory and formed the fifth province of Ireland. In 1543, under Henry VIII, Meath was partitioned and became East Meath and West Meath. The partition was almost certainly for the purpose of administration and the granting of additional baronies. Located as it was, in the centre of the country it earned the simple yet highly descriptive name *An Mhí* – the middle. Another explanation is to be found in D. P. W. Joyce's *A Child's History of Ireland* (1897). He states that the province of Meath was formed by cutting a *méidhe*, meaning 'neck', from each of the other provinces. The four pieces met at a place called *Aiall na Meeran* – 'The Stone of the Divisions' – at Ushnagh in County Westmeath. East Meath eventually became known as Meath.

BARONIES:

Athlone South – Brawney – Clonlonan – Corkaree – Delvin – Farbill – Fartullagh – Fore – Kilkenny West – Moyashel and Magheradernon – Moycashel – Moygoish – Rathconrath.

MOST COMMON NAMES:

O'Murtagh – Nugent – Fitzsimon – Dease – O'Curry – O'Melaghlin – O'Growney – McCarran – Dillon – Dalton – O'Daly – McAuley – McGee – O'Coffey – Tyrell – McGeoghegan – O'Carberry.

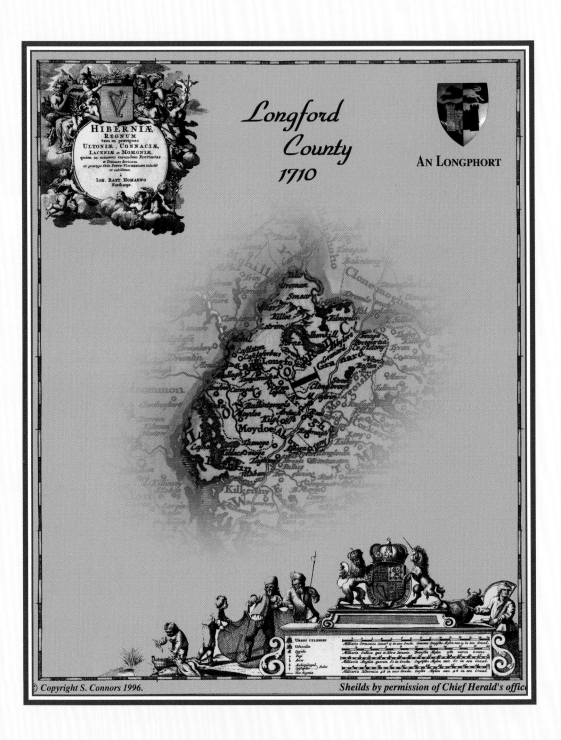

Longford
County
1710

AN LONGPHORT

HIBERNIÆ
REGNUM
tam in præcipuas
ULTONIÆ, CONNACIÆ,
LACENIÆ et MOMONIÆ,
quam in minores earundem Provincias
et Ditiones divisum,
ex prototypo GUIL. PETIT VINCREIANO deductili
et exhibitum
à
IOH. BATT HOMANNO
Norberge.

Sheilds by permission of Chief Herald's office

AN LONGFOIRT / LONGFORD

MEANING OF COUNTY NAME:

Longford in the Irish language is *An Longfoirt* – a term which signifies a fortress or encampment. The town of Longford was called in old documents 'Longford–O'Farrell' from the castle of the O'Farrells and the name was eventually applied to the county.

BARONIES:

Ardagh – Granard – Longford – Moydow – Rathcline – Shrule.

MOST COMMON NAMES:
McMaster – Gaynor – Leavy – O'Murtagh – Quinn – O'Mulroy – Flood – O'Farrell.

Antrim County 1710

AONTROIM

Sheilds by permission of Chief Herald's office

Aontroim / Antrim

MEANING OF COUNTY NAME:

An ancient rendering of this name was 'Oentrebh'. Although the spelling changed slightly the meaning was unaffected – 'Oen' became *aon* meaning literally 'one' and 'Trebh' changed to *Troim* meaning 'house' or 'tribe'. The name refers then to 'One House or Tribe'. It is unclear which tribe exactly is referred to. Another obscure and puzzling reference to Antrim occurs in *Illustrations of Irish History*. It reads as follows: *'Dubourdieu following the editor of Ware says, "the name is said to have been Andruim or Endruim – that is The Habitation of the Waters – from its being almost insulated by sea and lake".'*

BARONIES:

Antrim Lower – Antrim Upper – Belfast Lower – Belfast Upper – Cary – Castlereagh Upper – Dunluce Lower – Dunluce Upper – Glenarm Lower – Glenarm Upper – Kilconway – Massereene Lower – Massereene Upper – Toome Lower – Toome Upper.

MOST COMMON NAMES:

McQuillan – McCleary – O'Hara – O'Quinn – McDonnell – McKeown – McNeill – O'Hood – McAlister – O'Lynn – Lynch – O'Lavery.

Armagh
County
1710

ARD MHACHA

Sheilds by permission of Chief Herald's office

ARD MHACHA / ARMAGH

MEANING OF COUNTY NAME:

Armagh in the Irish language is *Ard Mhacha* which means 'The High Place of Macha'. In various ancient writings concerning the area three women are put forward as possible contenders: 1 – Macha, wife of Nevvy, said to have led a colony here after the deluge; 2 – Macha of the Golden Hair who founded the palace of Emania 300 years before Christianity and, 3 – Macha, wife of Crunn, who lived in the reign of Conor Mac Nessa in the first century. The second Macha was the most celebrated of the three and is said to be buried here. The place was probably named after her, which gives it a history of over 2,000 years.

BARONIES:

Armagh – Fews Lower – Fews Upper – Oneilland East – Oneilland West – Orior Lower – Orior Upper – Tiranny.

MOST COMMON NAMES:

O'Keelaghan – McCann – McSherry – O'Heron – O'Garvey – O'Loughran – O'Rogan – O'Hanlon – O'Hare – McGivern – McNally – O'Langan – McCone – McEntee – McPartlan – O'Mulcreevy – O'Hoey – McVeagh – O'Heany – McCourt – McBarron – O'Gowan.

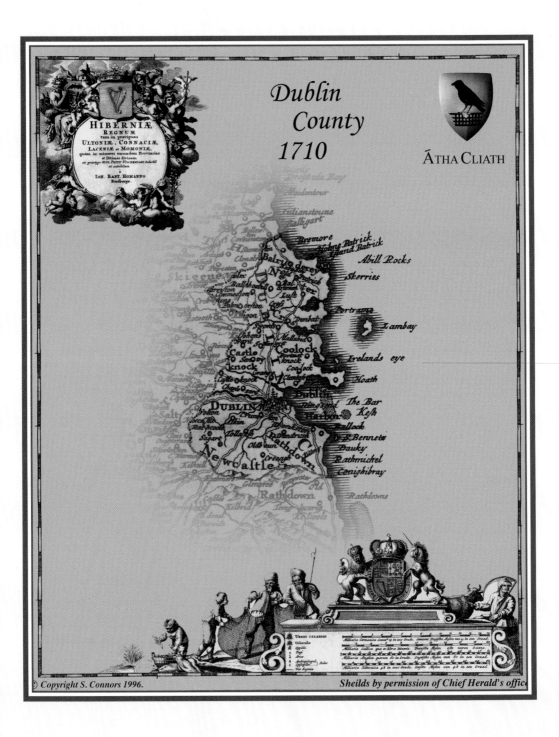

Dublin
County
1710

HIBERNIÆ
REGNUM
tam in præcipuas
ULTONIÆ, CONNACIÆ,
LACENIÆ et MOMONIÆ,
quam in minores earundem Provincias
et Ditiones divisum
ex prototypo GUIL. PETTY VICHEREANI deductil
et exhibitum
â
IOH. BAPT. HOMANNO
Noribergæ.

ÁTHA CLIATH

Sheilds by permission of Chief Herald's office

ÁTHA CLIATH / DUBLIN

MEANING OF COUNTY NAME:

Dublin was written in ancient times as *Duibh Linn* meaning 'black pool'. In an ancient document 'The Latin Life of St Kevin', it translated as *Nigra Therma* again meaning black pool. This was the name for the location of a foot-crossing over the Liffey. The crossing point itself was known in Irish as *Áth Cliath* ('ford of the hurdles') and was later applied to the city and then the county.

BARONIES:

Balrothery East – Balrothery West – Castleknock – Coolock – Dublin – Nethercross – Newcastle – Rathdown – Uppercross.

MOST COMMON NAMES:

Cruise – O'Casey – Delahyde – Plunkett – Talbot – Seagrave – Sarsfield – Bagot – Harold – O'Ronan.

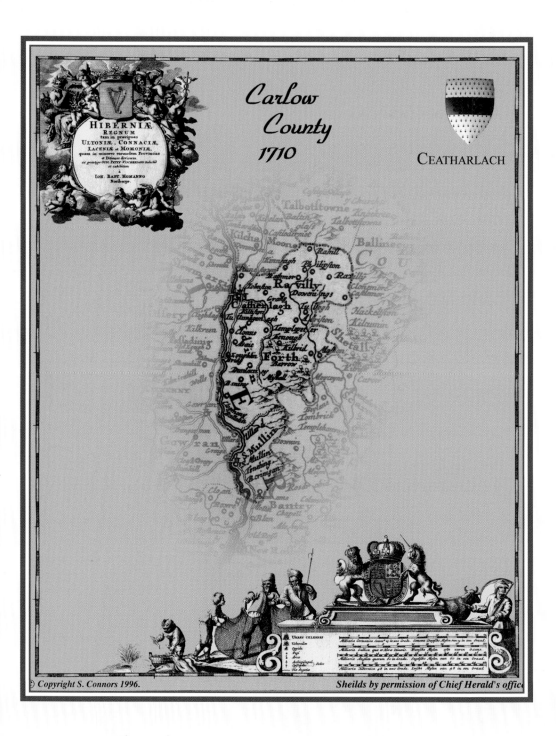

Carlow
County
1710

HIBERNIÆ
REGNUM
tam in praecipuas
ULTONIÆ, CONNACIÆ,
LAGENIÆ et MOMONIÆ,
quam in minores earundem Provincias
et Ditiones divisum
ex probtypo GUIL. PETTY VISCHERARD deductum
et cælatum
a
IOH. BAPT. HOMANNO
Noriberge.

CEATHARLACH

Sheilds by permission of Chief Herald's office

Ceatharlach / Carlow

MEANING OF COUNTY NAME:

Carlow in the Irish language is *Ceatharlach* meaning 'Four Lakes'. The River Barrow is believed to have formed four lakes near Carlow town at one time although no trace of them now remains. Early English writers referred to it as 'Catherlogh' or 'Katherlogh'.

BARONIES:

Carlow – Forth – Idrone East – Idrone West – Rathvilly – St Mullins Lower – St Mullins Upper – Slievemargy.

MOST COMMON NAMES:

Tallon – O'Nolan – O'Hayden – O'Neill – O'Ryan – O'Fortin (Fortune) – Kinsella.

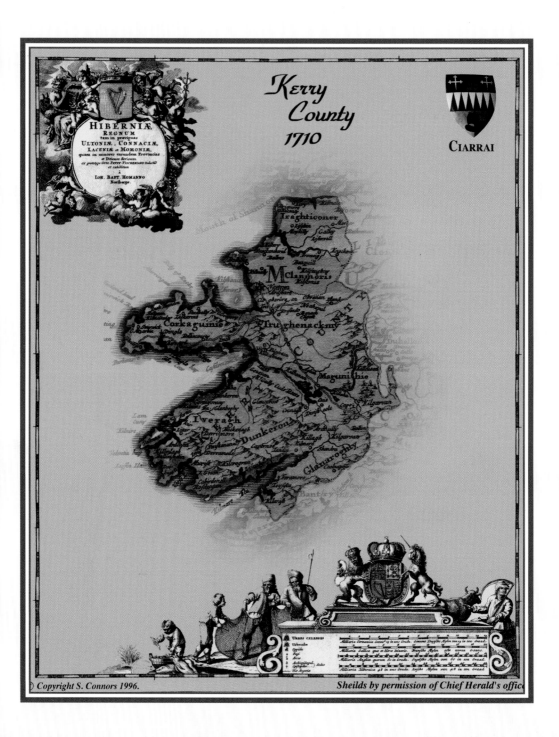

Kerry
County
1710

CIARRAI

HIBERNIÆ
REGNUM
tam in præcipuas
ULTONIÆ, CONNACIÆ,
LACENIÆ et MOMONIÆ,
quam in minores earundem Provincias
et Ditiones divisum
ex prototypo GUIL PETTY-VISCHERIANO reducto
et exhibitum
à
ION. BAPT. HOMANNO
Noribergæ.

Sheilds by permission of Chief Herald's office

CIARRAÍ / KERRY

MEANING OF COUNTY NAME:

'Ciar' was one of the three sons of Fergus – an ancient King of Ulster, and Maeve – Queen of Connacht. Each son was a leader of a tribe of people. Ciar settled in Munster in an area between Tralee and the Shannon. This tribe was known as the 'Ciarraidhe', i.e., The Race of Ciar. The name was applied to the district and eventually to the county. It was later anglicised to Kerry.

BARONIES:

Clanmaurice – Corkaguiny – Dunkerron North – Dunkerron South – Glanarought – Iraghticonnor – Iveragh – Magunihy – Trughanacmy.

MOST COMMON NAMES:

O'Connor – Kerry – Fitzmaurice – Fitzgerald – Stack – Ferriter – O'Long – O'Falvey – O'Shea – O'Moriarty – Galvin – McSweeney – O'Kelliher – O'Donoghue – Lynch – McCrohan – O'Sugrue – Mc-Elligott – O'Brosnan – O'Rahilly.

Kilkenny
County
1710

HIBERNIÆ
REGNUM
tam in præcipuas
ULTONIÆ, CONNACIÆ,
LACENIÆ et MOMONIÆ,
quam in minores earundem Provincias
et Ditiones divisim
ex prototypo GUIL. PETTY-FITGERARDO deducto
et exhibitum
a
IOH. BAPT. HOMANNO
Norimbergæ.

CILL CHAINNIGH

Sheilds by permission of Chief Herald's office

CILL CHAINNIGH / KILKENNY

MEANING OF COUNTY NAME:

Derives from the Irish word *Cill* meaning church (from the Latin *Cella)*. Kilkenny in Irish is *Cill Chainnaig* – The Church of St Cainnech or Canice – AD 517 – 600.

BARONIES:

Callan – Crannagh – Fassadinan – Galmoy – Gowran – Ida – Iverk – Kells – Kilculliheen – Knocktopher – Shillelogher.

MOST COMMON NAMES:

McGillpatrick – O'Brennan – Cody – Butler – Cantwell – Grace – Comerford – O'Clery – O'Shea – Rothe – Archer – Barron – Sweetman – O'Dunphy – O'Phelan – Forrestal – O'Queally – McBreen – O'Carroll – Shortall – O'Broder.

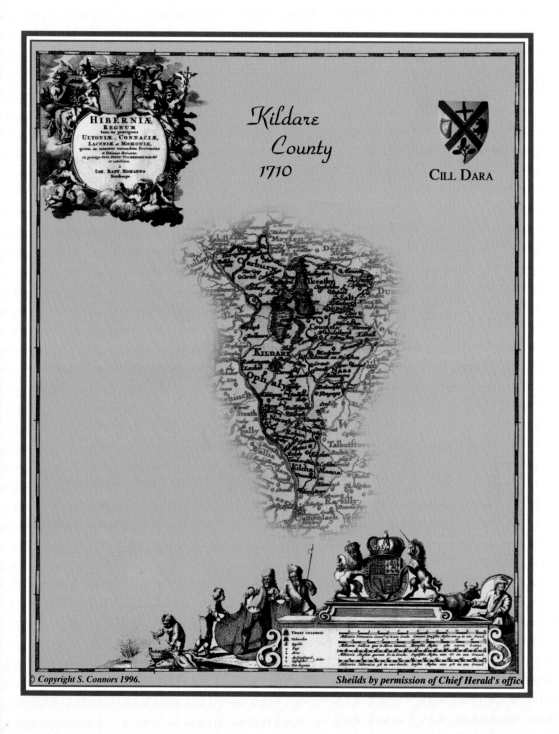

Kildare
County
1710

CILL DARA

Sheilds by permission of Chief Herald's offic

CILL DARA / KILDARE

ORIGIN OF COUNTY NAME:

According to a tale in the *Book of Leinster* the area was originally called *Druim Criaidh* possibly meaning The Hill or Ridge of the Large Branchy Tree (from the Irish words *Drum* meaning back and *Craobh* meaning branch or large branchy tree). There was, by all accounts, a very notable oak tree growing there, near which St Brigid built her cell. This was called in Irish *Cill Dara* meaning the Church of the Oak and was later anglicised to Kildare.

BARONIES:

Carbury – Clane – Connell – Ikeathy and Oughterany – Kilcullen – Kilkea and Moone – Naas North – Naas South – Narragh and Reban East – Narragh and Reban West – Offaly East – Offaly West – Salt North – Salt South.

MOST COMMON NAMES:

Fitzgerald – Eustace – Birmingham – White – Wogan – O'Byrne – O'Morohan – O'Cullen.

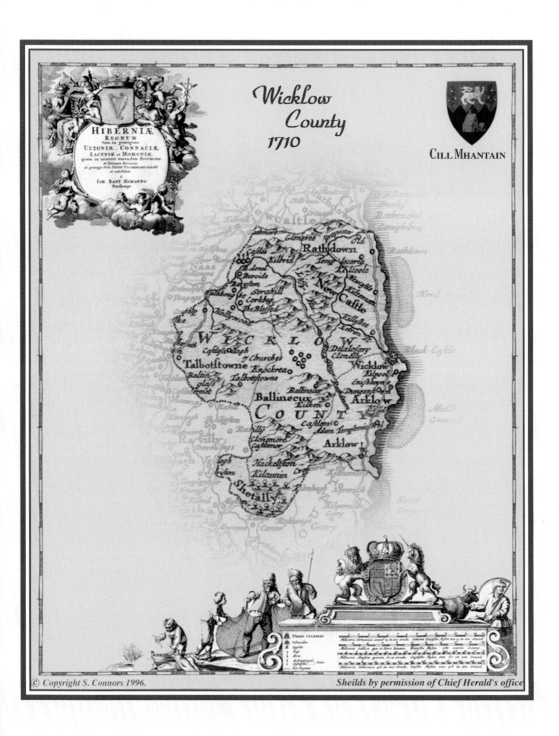

Wicklow
County
1710

CILL MHANTAIN

HIBERNIÆ
REGNUM
tam in præcipuas
ULTONIÆ, CONNACIÆ,
LACENIÆ et MOMONI�æ,
quam in minores eiusdem Provincias
et Ditiones divisum,
et penique cum Pavti Vlisssiratis indicatú
et exhibitum
à
IOH. BAPT ROMANNO
Northorpe

Sheilds by permission of Chief Herald's office

CILL MHANTÁIN / WICKLOW

MEANING OF COUNTY NAME:

It is possible that the name derived from the Norwegians as the old spellings sometimes began with 'Wyk' or 'Wyg' which may hint at the Scandinavian 'Vig' meaning a bay. Wicklow in the Irish language is *Cill Mhantáin* – St Mantan's Church. St Mantan was said to have been one of St Patrick's companions who lost his front teeth in a skirmish with the natives when first landing at Wicklow. He became known as Manton meaning toothless. In some areas the word *mantach* is used to describe someone who has lost their front teeth.

BARONIES:

Arklow – Ballinacor North – Ballinacor South – Newcastle – Rathdown – Shillelagh – Talbotstown Lower – Talbotstown Upper.

MOST COMMON NAMES:

Cosgrave – O'Teige – O'Toole – O'Kelly – O'Byrne.

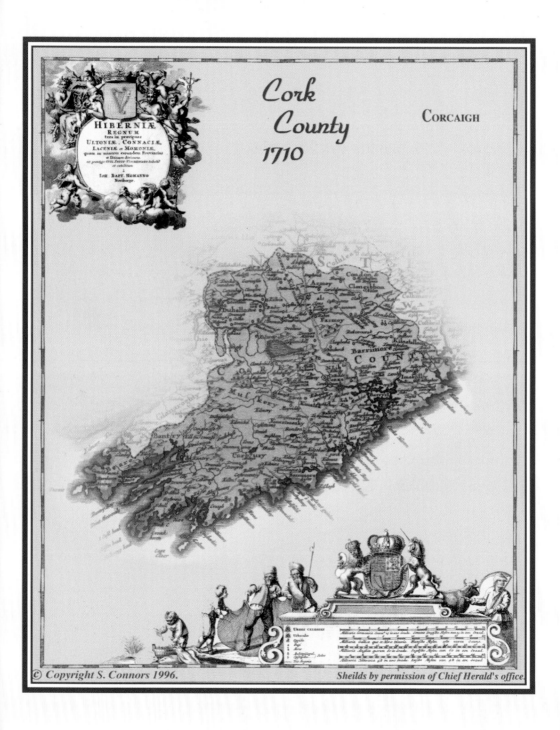

Cork
County
1710

CORCAIGH

HIBERNIÆ
REGNUM
tam in præcipuas
ULTONIÆ, CONNACIÆ,
LAGENIÆ et MOMONIÆ,
quam in minores earundem Provincias
et Dinaces divisum
ex prototypo Guil. Petty Viceprætoris subsd
et exhibitum
à
IOH. BAPT. HOMANNO
Noribergæ.

CORCAIGH / CORK

MEANING OF COUNTY NAME:

The name derives from *corcach* meaning a swamp or marshy ground.
In the sixth century St Finbar founded a monastery on the mouth of
the river Lee. The settlement that grew up was plundered many times
by the Danes or 'Ostmen' before they themselves settled on this inhos-
pitable site. The swampy area was known as *An Corcach Mór* – The
Great Swamp or *Corcach Mór Mumhann* – The Great Marsh of Munster.

BARONIES:

Bantry – Condon – Barrymore – Bear – Carbery East (E.D.) – Carbery
East (W.D.) – Carbery West (E.D.) – Carbery West (W.D.) – Condons
and Clangibbon – Cork – Courceys – Duhallo – Fermoy – Ibane and
Barrymore – Imokilly – Kerrycurrihy – Kinalea – Kinalineary – Kin-
natalloon – Kinsale – Muskerry East – Muskerry West – Orrery and
Kilmore.

MOST COMMON NAMES:

Barry – Condon – Lombard – Roche – Nagle – Barrett – Nugent –
Skiddy – Gould – De Courcey – McSherry – McAuliffe – O'Keeffe –
O'Riordan – McSweeney – O'Callaghan – McCarthy – O'Regan –
O'Donovan – O'Driscoll – Collins – O'Mahony – Coakley – O'Daly –
Harrington – Lyons – O'Flynn – O'Shelly.

Derry
County
1710

HIBERNIÆ
REGNUM
tam in præcipuas
ULTONIÆ, CONNACIÆ,
LACHNIÆ et MOMONIÆ,
quam in minores earundem Provincias
et Dittoeses divisum,
ex prototypo sive PETTY-VELCHELIANO deductâ
et exhibitum
à
IOH. BAPT. HOMANNO
Noribergæ.

DOIRE

Sheilds by permission of Chief Herald's office

DOIRE / DERRY

MEANING OF COUNTY NAME:

Derry is the anglicised version of the Irish word *Doire* meaning an oak wood. The area, like much of Ireland, must have been rich in natural oak forest for the name to remain and be applied to the county.

BARONIES:

Coleraine – Liberties of Coleraine North-East – Keenaght – Londonderry – Liberties of Londonderry North-East – Loughinsholin – Tirkeeran.

MOST COMMON NAMES:

McGilligan – O'Mullan – O'Connor – McClosky – O'Deery – McColgan – McCrilly – O'Dimond – O'Carolan – O'Mulvenna – McCracken – O'Hegarty – O'Mulhollan – McRory – O'Corr – O'Kelly – McGurk – O'Cahan.

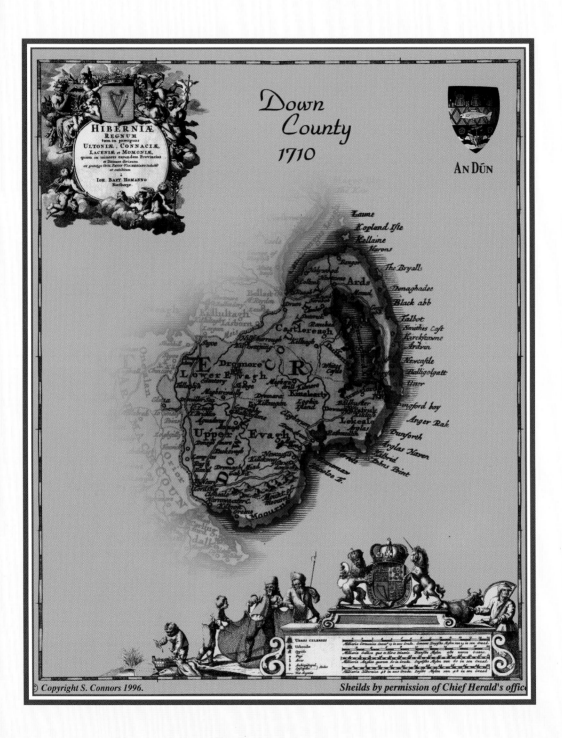

Down
County
1710

An Dún

Sheilds by permission of Chief Herald's office

An Dún / Down

MEANING OF COUNTY NAME:

The word *Dún* has always been applied to the great forts, with a high central mound, flat at the top and surrounded by several – usually three – earthen walls. County Down takes its name from the large entrenched fort which was situated in the town of Downpatrick. In the first century this fortress was the residence of a warrior of the Red Branch Knights called Celtchair or Keltar of the Battles. Over the ages it had been variously called Dunkeltar, Rathkeltar and Áraskeltar (*Áras* means a habitation). The latter part of the name was eventually dropped leaving the word Dún which passed into the Latin *Dunum* and finally into the present name Down.

BARONIES:

Ards Lower – Ards Upper – Castlereagh Lower – Castlereagh Upper – Dufferin – Iveagh Lower, Lower Half – Iveagh Lower, Upper Half – Iveagh Upper, Lower Half – Iveagh Upper, Upper Half – Kinelarty – Lecale Lower – Lecale Upper – Mourne – Lordship of Newry – Orior Upper.

MOST COMMON NAMES:

O'Neill – O'Mulcreevy – McGilmore – Savage – McMurry – White – O'Lowry – O'Harvy – McDonegan – McGuinness – O'Rooney – O'Devaney.

Donegal
County
1710

DŪN NA nGALL

HIBERNIÆ
REGNUM
tam in præcipuas
ULTONIÆ, CONNACIÆ,
LACENIÆ et MOMONIÆ,
quam in minores earundem Provincias
et Ditiones divisum

IOH. BAPT. HOMANNO
Noriberga

Sheilds by permission of Chief Herald's office

Dún na nGall / Donegal

MEANING OF COUNTY NAME:

In the Irish language *Dún* means fortress and *Gall* means foreigners. Together they mean the Fortress of the Foreigners. These foreigners were most probably Danes who would have erected a *Dún* or fortress there. The name of the site was later applied to the county.

BARONIES:

Banagh – Boylagh – Inishowen East – Inishowen West – Kilmacrenan – Raphoe South – Raphoe North – Tirhugh.

MOST COMMON NAMES:

O'Kernaghan – McSweeney – O'Friel – Duffy – McGonigle – Begley – Coyle – McFadden – O'Boyle – O'Mooney – Gallagher – McMenamin – McNulty – McGrath – Ward – Clery – Hughes – Lynch – McLoughlin – McDevitt – O'Shiel – O'Donnell – McGlinchy.

Fermanagh
County
1710

HIBERNIÆ
REGNUM
tam in praecipuas
ULTONIÆ, CONNACIÆ,
LACENIÆ et MOMONIÆ,
quam in minores earundem Provincias
et Ditiones divisum
et prototypo GUIL. PETTY Watheriano Inducto
et exhibitum
à
IOH. BAPT. HOMANNO
Norinberge.

FIR MANACH

Sheilds by permission of Chief Herald's office

FEAR MANACH / FERMANAGH

MEANING OF COUNTY NAME:

Fermanagh was named after a Leinster chieftain named Monach who was fifth in line to Cahirmore, King of Ireland (120–123). Monach's entire tribe the 'Fir Monach' had to flee Leinster after killing Enna, son of the King of Leinster. Some of them settled in County Down where the name died out. Another branch settled on the shores of Lough Erne and eventually acquired a territory stretching over the entire county of Fermanagh. The tribal name was applied to the county and survives to the present day.

BARONIES:

Clanawley – Clankelly – Coole – Knockninny – Lurg – Magheraboy – Magherastephana – Tirkennedy.

MOST COMMON NAMES:

O'Slevin – O'Muldoon – McEntaggart – O'Corcoran – O'Bannon – O'Cassidy – Maguire – O'Devine – McKiernan – O'Hussey – Mc-Cullen – O'Breslin – McManus – McGilroy – McGarraghan – McDonnell – McCorry – McAuley – Keenan – McMulrooney – McCarbery – O'Keenan – O'Connolly – O'Scanlon – O'Corrigan – O'Flanagan – McGoldrick.

Galway
County
1710

GAILLIMH

HIBERNIÆ
REGNUM
tam in præcipuas
ULTONIÆ, CONNACIÆ,
LACENIÆ et MOMONIÆ,
quam in minores earundem Provincias
et Ditiones divisum
et pretiqe Gul. Petty Equelborum tradidit
et exhibet
à
IOH. BAPT. HOMANNO
Norimbergæ

Sheilds by permission of Chief Herald's office

Gaillimh / Galway

MEANING OF COUNTY NAME:

There are two possibilities for the origin of the name Galway. The first is that it is named after a Celtic princess named Galvia – the daughter of Breasil, King of the Firbolgs – who was drowned in an area of the river called 'Galvia's Rock'. This seems less likely than the following account. Galway, until it was invaded by Anglo-Normans in 1232, was known by the native Irish as *Baile na Shruthán* which meant 'The Town of the Streams'. The Irish word *Gaillimh* – literally translated as foreigners – was applied to the town after the invasion to mean 'The Town of the Foreigners' and remains to the present day. The word *Gaillimh* is said to derive from *Gall* the name given to any foreigner. The word *Gall* is thought to derive from 'Gauls', lending weight to the theory that there was an early French settlement on these shores.

BARONIES:

Aran – Athenry – Ballymoe – Ballynahinch – Clare – Clonmacnowen – Galway – Kilconnell – Killian – Kiltartan – Leitrim – Loughrea – Moycarn – Moycullen – Ross – Tiaquin – Dunkellin – Dunmore – Longford.

MOST COMMON NAMES:

McConneely – Joyce – O'Devaney – O'Flaherty – McHenry – O'Moran – Bermingham – McEgan – O'Conor Don – O'Mullan – O'Mannion – Lyons – McRedmond (Burke) – O'Feeney – O'Kelly – O'Faherty – O'Touhy – O'Daly – O'Naughton – O'Shaughnessy – O'Madden – O'Mahon – McEgan – O'Ruane – O'Horan – O'Cahill – O'Tracy – Forde.

Laois
County
1710

LAOISE

HIBERNIÆ
REGNUM
tam in præcipuas
ULTONIÆ, CONNACIÆ,
LACENIÆ et MOMONIÆ,
quam in minores earundem Provincias
et Ditiones divisum,
ex genuinæ Gul. Petty Fitzgeraldo habeo
et exhibitum
à
IOH. BAPT. HOMANNO
Norimberge.

Laois / Leix

Meaning of county name:

In the reign of 'Felimy the Lawgiver' AD 111–119, the men of Munster seized the ancient territory of Ossory and all the territories of Leinster as far as Mullaghmast. Eventually they were expelled by an Ulster chief named Lughaidh Laeighseach, son of Laeighseach Canvore, son of the renowned Conall Cearnach, chief of the Red Branch Knights of Ulster. For this service the King of Leinster granted Lughaidh a territory there. His descendants, the O'Moores inherited from him the tribe name Laeighis (phon. Leesh) and the territory took the same name. It was commonly written as Leix. The name all but disappeared for a time and the county was called Queen's County. (A statute passed in 1556 relating to the territories of Laois and Offaly read: ' ... *Be it enacted that the King and Queen, and the heirs and successors of the Queen, shall have, hold, and possess for ever, as in the right of the Crown of England and Ireland, the said countries of Leix, Slewmargy, Irry, Glenmaliry, and Offaly'.)* Today, although spelled differently, it is again known by its ancient name.

Baronies:

Ballyadams – Clanconagh – Glarmallagh – Cullenagh – Upperwoods – Maryborough East – Maryborough West – Portnahinch – Slievemargy – Stradbally – Tinnahinch.

Most common names:

O'Dempsey – O'Regan – O'Dunn – O'Doran – McEvoy – O'Duff – O'Lawlor – O'Keally (Kelly) – O'Delaney – O'More (Moore) – O'Dowling – O'Tracey – O'Devoy – O'Mulhall – McCashin – O'Brophey – O'Deegan – O'Tynan – McCostigan.

Leitrim
County
1710

LIATROIM

Shields by permission of Chief Herald's office

LIATROIM / LEITRIM

MEANING OF COUNTY NAME:

Many placenames in Ireland incorporate the word *druim* which literally translates to 'back'. In this context *druim* would signify a natural ridge in the land; e.g., *Druim fhada* would mean 'Long ridge'. In some areas the 'd' sound softened over the years to a 't' sound. This is the case with Leitrim, the full name of which derives from *Liath-dhruim* meaning 'Grey ridge'. It is now spelt *Liatroim* or Leitrim in the English.

BARONIES:

Carrigallen – Drumshaire – Leitrim – Mohill – Rosclogher.

MOST COMMON NAMES:

O'Meehan – McGoldrick – McClancy – O'Rourke – O'Curneen – Ford – McCoogan – McSharry – Early – McMorrow – O'Mulvey – Reynolds – McShanley – Gilroy – McGourtey.

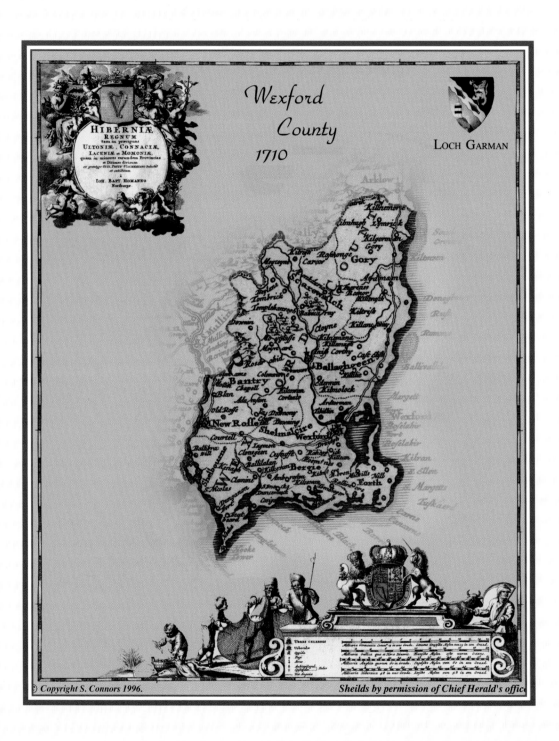

Wexford County 1710

LOCH GARMAN

Sheilds by permission of Chief Herald's office

LOCH GARMAN / WEXFORD

ORIGIN OF COUNTY NAME:

Wexford, like Waterford, is one of only a few Irish names which is either wholly or partly Danish in origin. The 'ford' part of the name derives from the Danish word *fjiord* meaning an inlet into the sea. Early English writers referred to it as 'Weisford' with the 'weis' part changing slightly to the name we use today.

BARONIES:

Ballaghkeen North – Ballaghkeen South – Bantry – Bargy – Ida – Gorey – Forth – Scarawalsh – Shelbourne – Shelmaliere West.

MOST COMMON NAMES:

O'Doyle – McKeogh – McDavymore – O'Bolger – O'Broder – O'Lynan – Kinsella – McMorrough – O'Hartly – Redmond – Walsh – Hayes – Masterson – Sinnot – Corish – Hoare – Devereux – Keating – Rossiter – Furlong – Stafford – Laffan.

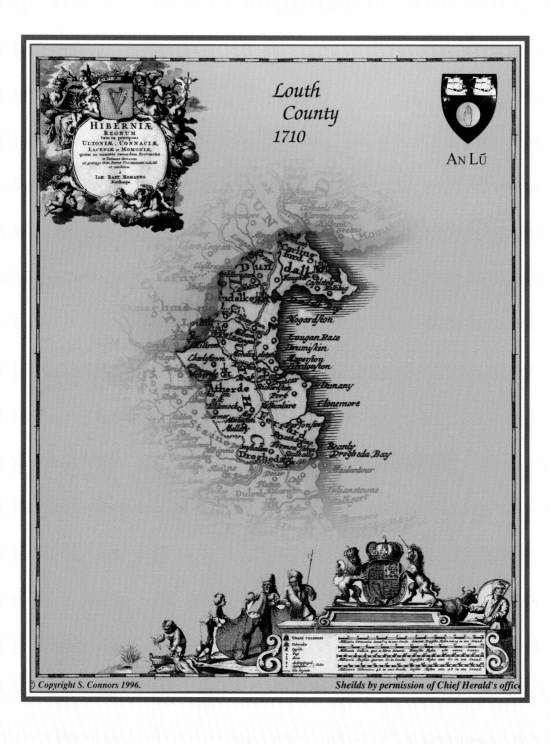

Louth
County
1710

An Lū

HIBERNIÆ
REGNUM
tam in præcipuas
ULTONIÆ, CONNACIÆ,
LACENIÆ et MOMONIÆ,
quam in minores earundem Provincias
et Ditiones divisum.
ex prototypo GUIL. PETTY Hibernaro deductâ
et exhibitum
à
IOH. BAPT. HOMANNO
Noribergæ.

Sheilds by permission of Chief Herald's office

Lú / Louth

MEANING OF COUNTY NAME:

The original meaning of Louth is not certain. It is thought to derive from the Irish word *Lugh* or *Lughmhaigh* meaning a hollow or plane. This would be consistent with the ancient practice of allowing the geographical features of an area determine its name.

BARONIES:

Ardee – Drogheda – Duleek Lower – Dundalk Lower – Dundalk Upper – Ferrard – Louth.

MOST COMMON NAMES:

McSolly – Verdon – Bellew – Taaffe – O'Carroll – Dowdall – Moore – Plunkett.

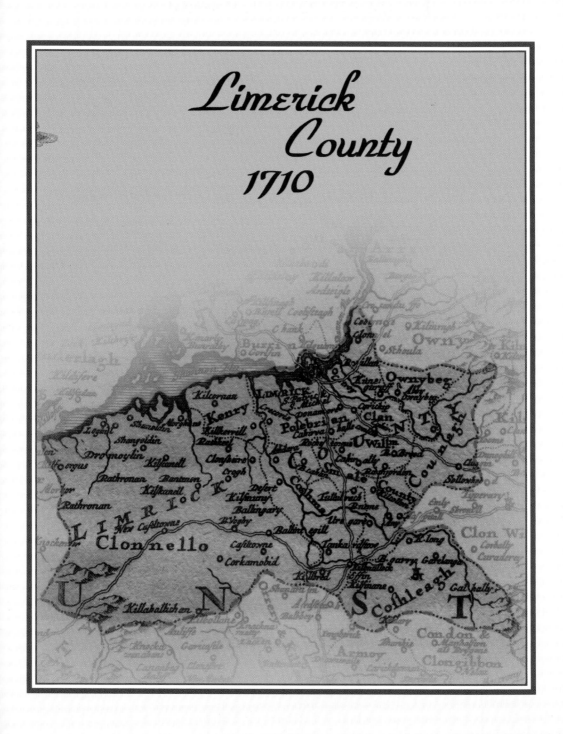

Limerick
County
1710

LUIMNEACH / LIMERICK

ORIGIN OF COUNTY NAME:

Luimneach in Irish derives from the Irish word *Lom* meaning bare. The full name means a bare or barren spot of land. This was the name of the area long before the foundation of the city.

BARONIES:

Clanwilliam – Clonello Lower – Clonello Upper – Coonagh – Coshlea – Coshma – Glenquin – Kenry – Kilmallock – Pubblebrian – Shanid – Smallcounty – North Liberties.

MOST COMMON NAMES:

Fitzgerald – Fitzgibbon – Wall – Neville – O'Mulholland – McKeogh – Browne – O'Kirby – de Lacey – O'Mackessy – O'Kinnealy – O'Heffernan – O'Flannery.

LUIMNEACH

Mayo
County
1710

MAIGH EO

Sheilds by permission of Chief Herald's office

MAIGH EO / MAYO

MEANING OF COUNTY NAME:

In the seventh century, St Colman, having retired from the See of Lindisfarne, returned to Ireland and founded a monastery at a place called *Magh Eo* – The Plain of the Yews. The name was eventually applied to the entire county.

BARONIES:

Burrishoole – Carra – Clanmorris – Costello – Erris – Gallen – Kilmaine – Murrisk – Ross – Tirawley – Tireragh.

MOST COMMON NAMES:

Hayes – O'Ronan – O'Towney – McHale – O'Moran – Leonard – O'Murray – O'Clery – O'Mangan – O'Finan – McAndrew – Jordan – Conway – Barrett – O'Malley – Loftus – O'Flannery – Brogan – O'Dowd – Burke – Prendergast – Costello – McNicholas – O'Carney – O'Tierny – Quigley – O'Flynn – O'Dugan – Garvey – Conway.

Meath
County
1710

HIBERNIÆ
REGNUM
tam in præcipuas
ULTONIÆ, CONNACIÆ,
LACENIÆ et MOMONIÆ,
quam in minores earundem Provincias
et Ditiones divisum
ex prototypo Guil. Petty Vicheriano deductus
et exhibitus
à
Ioh. Bapt. Homanno
Norinbergæ.

An Mhí

Sheilds by permission of Chief Herald's office

An Mhí / Meath

MEANING OF COUNTY NAME:

There are two possible meanings for the name of Meath. The first and most commonly accepted is that the Irish word *mí* literally translates as the middle or the middle place. Meath and Westmeath was originally one territory and formed the fifth province of Ireland. Located as it was in the centre of the country it earned the simple yet highly descriptive name *An Mhí* – the middle. The other explanation is to be found in D. P. W. Joyce's *Child's History of Ireland*. He states that the province of Meath was formed by cutting a *meidhe* meaning 'neck' from each of the other provinces. The four pieces met at a place called *Aiall na Meeran* – 'The Stone of the Divisions' – at Ushnagh in County Westmeath.

BARONIES:

Deece Lower – Deece Upper – Duleek Lower – Duleek Upper – Dunboyne – Fore – Kells Lower – Kells Upper – Lune – Morgallion – Moyfenrath Lower – Moyfenrath Upper – Navan Lower – Navan Upper – Ratoath – Skreen – Slane Lower – Slane Upper.

MOST COMMON NAMES:

O'Loughnane – Fleming – O'Carolan – O'Mulhollan – O'Devane – Peppard – O'Reilly – Cusack – Hayes – Dillon – Dowdall – Preston – O'Hennessy – Plunkett – Nangle – Quinlan – O'Kelly – Eagan – Hussey – McGogarty – O'Connolly – Darcy.

Monaghan
County
1710

MUINEACHÁN

Sheilds by permission of Chief Herald's office

MUINEACHÁN / MONAGHAN

MEANING OF COUNTY NAME:

The name Monaghan probably derives from the Irish word *Muine* meaning a brake or a shrubbery. Its Irish name is *Muineachán* which, when directly translated, means 'Little Shrubbery'.

BARONIES:

Cremorne – Dartree – Farney – Monaghan – Trough.

MOST COMMON NAMES:

McNally – McAneeny – Cosgrave – McMahon – McTeige – McEntee – O'Callan – Brannagan – Larkin – McArdle – O'Connolly – O'Donegan – Finn – Hayes.

Waterford
County
1710

HIBERNIÆ
REGNUM
tam in præcipuas
ULTONIÆ, CONNACIÆ,
LACENIÆ et MOMONIÆ,
quam in minores earundem Provincias
et Ditiones divisum
ex prototypo GUIL.PETTY-VISCHERIANO (reducto)
et exhibitum
à
IOH. BAPT. HOMANNO
Noribergæ.

PORT LAIRGE

PORT LÁIRGE / WATERFORD

MEANING OF COUNTY NAME:

Waterford appears to be one of only a few county names which is either partly or wholly Danish in origin. Referred to as 'Vadrefiord' by early English writers – *fjiord* being the Danish word for an inlet into the sea.

BARONIES:

Coshmore and Coshbride – Decies within Drum – Decies without Drum – Gaultiere – Kilculliheen – Middle Third – Upper Third – Glenahiry.

MOST COMMON NAMES:

Power – Henebry – Wyse – McGrath – O'Phelan – O'Crotty – Ormonde – O'Keane – O'Brien – O'Brick.

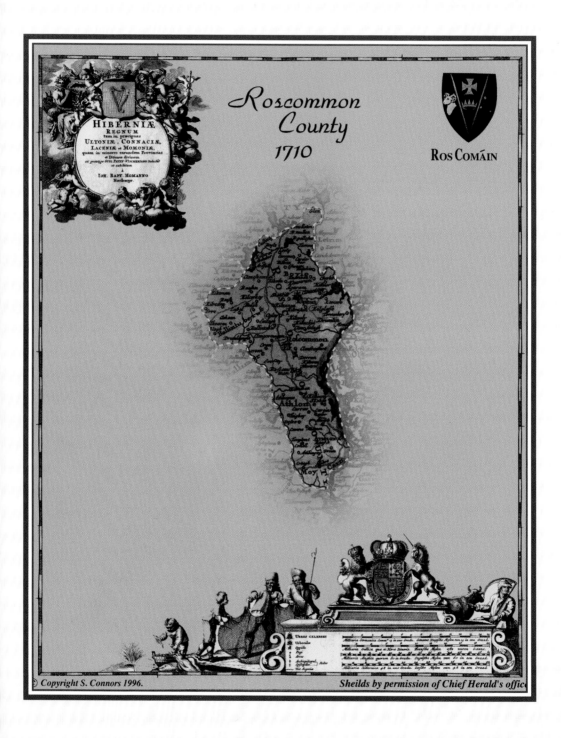

Roscommon County
1710

HIBERNIÆ
REGNUM
tam in. principuas
ULTONIÆ, CONNACIÆ,
LACENIÆ et MOMONIÆ,
quam in minores earundem Provincias
et Ditiones divisum
et prototype GUIL PETTY VIcKERIANO Inductis
et exhibitum
à
IOH. BAPT. HOMANNO
Noribergæ.

ROS COMÁIN

Sheilds by permission of Chief Herald's office

Ros Comáin / Roscommon

MEANING OF COUNTY NAME:

Ros has several meanings in Irish one of which is 'wood'. Roscommon is named after St Coman who founded a monastery there. Literally translated it means St Coman's Wood. According to the *Four Masters*, St Coman died around AD 746 or 747 although other authorities place him much later.

BARONIES:

Athlone North – Ballintober North – Ballintober South – Ballymoe – Boyle – Castlereagh – Costello – Frenchpark – Moycarn – Roscommon.

MOST COMMON NAMES:

O'Lavin – O'Molloy – O'Mullaney – O'Feeheny – French – O'Giblin – McGreevy – McWeeney – O'Beirne – O'Duignan – McMonaghan – McManus – O'Mulvihill – O'Connellan – O'Conor Rua – O'Rattigan – O'Duffy – O'Mulconry – McQuilly – O'Hanley – Hayes – O'Flynn – O'Murphy – McAneeny – O'Mulrenan – O'Mulkerin – McDowell – O'Conor Don – McGeraghty – McGlynn – O'Mulready – O'Furey – O'Casey – O'Murray – O'Fallon – McKeogh – O'Mulkerron – O'Naughton.

Sligo
County
1710

SLIGEAGH

HIBERNIÆ
REGNUM
tam in præcipuas
ULTONIÆ, CONNACIÆ,
LACENIÆ et MOMONIÆ
quam in minores earundem Provincias
et Ditiones divisum
ex prototypo GUIL. PETTY Knightmaroni deducta
et exhibita
a
IOH. BAPT. HOMANNO
Norimberg.

Sheilds by permission of Chief Herald's office

Sligeach / Sligo

MEANING OF COUNTY NAME:

The River Garavogue which runs through Sligo Town was originally called *Slígeach* meaning 'Shelly River'. This name was applied to the town and later to the county before being anglicised to Sligo.

BARONIES:

Carbury – Coolavin – Corran – Leyny – Tireragh – Tirerrill.

MOST COMMON NAMES:

O'Hart – O'Boland – O'Finn – O'Scannell – O'Noone – McErlean – O'Spelman – O'Meeney – O'Rafferty – O'Loughery – O'Dowd – O'Tarpey – White – McAlary – O'Hara – McDonagh – Conway – McBreheny – McDurkan – O'Higgins – O'Devlin – O'Mohan.

Tipperary
County
1710

TIOBRAID ARANN

Sheilds by permission of Chief Herald's office

TIOBRAID ÁRANN / TIPPERARY

MEANING OF COUNTY NAME:

Tobar meaning a water well in the Irish language was sometimes written as 'Tipper'. The well which gave its name to the town and then to the county is situated just off the main street of the town. In Irish it is known as *Tiobraid Arann* – the Well of Ara. Ara was the name of the ancient territory in which it is situated.

BARONIES:

Lower Ormond – Upper Ormond – Owney and Arra – Ikerrin – Kilnamanagh – Eliogarty – Clanwilliam – Middle Third – Slieveardagh – Iffa and Offa East – Iffa and Offa West – Glenahiry – Upper Third.

MOST COMMON NAMES:

O'Kennedy – O'Meagher – O'Brien – Mathew – Purcell – Burke – Prendergast – Ryan – O'Spillane – O'Fogarty – O'Lonergan – O'Dwyer – O'Cahill – Troy – O'Scully.

Tyrone
County
1710

TIR EOGHAIN

Sheilds by permission of Chief Herald's office

Tír Eoghain / Tyrone

MEANING OF COUNTY NAME:

In the Irish language the name *Tír Eoghain* literally means the country or territory of Eoghan. The Eoghan referred to was Eoghan O'Neill, one of the sons of Niall of the Nine Hostages who was High King of Ireland in the fifth century. Eoghan travelled north to find for himself a principality and settled in an area which originally included parts of Donegal, Derry and Armagh as well as Tyrone. His name was later applied to the county and anglicised to Tyrone.

BARONIES:

Clogher – Dungannon Lower – Dungannon Middle – Dungannon Upper – Omagh East – Omagh West – Strabane Lower – Strabane Upper.

MOST COMMON NAMES:

O'Quinney – O'Mellan – Hayes – McCreehan – O'Corry – O'Neill – O'Henry – McShane – McNamee – O'Laverty – O'Murphy – O'Donnelly – McCawell – McEtigan – O'Devlin – O'Hagan – O'Quinn – O'Hamil – McGinity – O'Tomelty – McGilmartin – O'Cahan.

Offaly
County
1710

HIBERNIÆ
REGNUM
tam in præcipuas
ULTONIÆ, CONNACIÆ,
LACENIÆ et MOMONIÆ,
quam in minores earundem Provincias
et Ditiones divisum
et prototypo GUIL. PETTY VISCHERIANO Inductus
et exhibitum
à
IOH. BAPT. HOMANNO
Norimbergæ.

UIBH FHÁILÍ

Sheilds by permission of Chief Herald's office

Uíbh Fhailí / Offaly

MEANING OF COUNTY NAME:

Cahirmór was monarch of Ireland AD 120–123. His eldest son was 'Ros Failghe' which meant Ros of the Rings. His descendants were called 'Hy Failghe' and possessed a large territory around Kildare, Laois and Offaly to which they gave their tribal name. Like Laois, which was named Queen's County for more than four hundred years, Offaly was renamed King's County. (A statute passed in 1556 relating to the territories of Laois and Offaly read: '... *Be it enacted that the King and Queen, and the heirs and successors of the Queen, shall have, hold, and possess for ever, as in the right of the Crown of England and Ireland, the said countries of Leix, Slewmargy, Irry, Glenmaliry, and Offaly'.*) The name still exists as Offaly which was applied to the county and to two baronies in Kildare.

BARONIES:

Ballyboy – Ballybritt – Ballycowan – Clonlisk – Coolestown – Eglish – Garrycastle – Geashill – Kilcoursey – Philipstown Upper – Philipstown Lower – Warrenstown.

MOST COMMON NAMES:

O'Caherny (Fox) – McEnkegrie (Lestrange) – O'Breene – O'Malone –

McCoghlan – O'Rigney – O'Flattery – McCoolahan – O'Mooney – O'Hennessy – McColgan – O'Cunneen – O'Fallon – O'Connor Faly – O'Behan – O'Bracken – O'Bergan – O'Molloy – O'Holohan – Delahunty – O'Flanagan – O'Dooley – Ely O'Carroll – O'Bannon – McGuilfoyle – McCorcoran – O'Riordan – O'Meagher.

INDEX OF FAMILY NAMES

McDurkan 79
McEgan 57
McElligott 39
McEnkegrie (Lestrange) 86
McEnright 25
McEntaggart 55
McEntee 33, 73
McErlean 79
McEtigan 83
McEvoy 59
McFadden 53
McGarraghan 55
McGee 27
McGeoghegan 27
McGeraghty 77
McGilligan 49
McGillpatrick 41
McGilmartin 83
McGilmore 51
McGilroy 55
McGinity 83
McGivern 33
McGlinchy 53
McGlynn 77
McGogarty 71
McGoldrick 55, 61
McGonigle 53
McGorman 25
McGourtey 61
McGovern 23
McGowan 23
McGrath 25, 53, 75
McGreevy 77
McGuilfoyle 86
McGuinness 51
McGurk 49
McHale 69
McHenry 57

McIlduff 23
McInerney 25
McKeane 25
McKeogh 63, 67, 77
McKeown 31
McKiernan 23, 55
McLoughlin 53
McMahon 25, 73
McManus 55, 77
McMaster 29
McMenamin 53
McMonoghan 77
McMorrough 63
McMorrow 61
McMulrooney 55
McMurry 51
McNally 33, 73
McNamara 25
McNamee 83
McNeill 31
McNicholas 69
McNulty 53
McPartlan 33
McQuillan 31
McQuilly 77
McRedmond (Burke) 57
McRory 49
McShane 83
McShanley 61
McSharry 61
McSheedy 25
McSherry 33, 47
McSolly 65
McSweeney 39, 47, 53
McTeige 73
McVeagh 33
McWeeney 77
Moore 65

O'Dowling 59
O'Doyle 63
O'Driscoll 47
O'Duff 59
O'Duffy 77
O'Dugan 69
O'Duignan 77
O'Dunn 59
O'Dunphy 41
O'Dwyer 81
O'Faherty 57
O'Fallon 77, 86
O'Falvey 39
O'Farrell 29
O'Farrelly 23
O'Feeheny 77
O'Feeney 57
O'Finan 69
O'Finn 79
O'Flaherty 57
O'Flanagan 55, 86
O'Flannery 67, 69
O'Flattery 86
O'Flynn 47, 69, 77
O'Fogarty 81
O'Fortin (Fortune) 37
O'Friel 53
O'Furey 77
O'Garvey 33
O'Giblin 77
O'Gowan 33
O'Growney 27
O'Hagan 83
O'Hamil 83
O'Hanley 77
O'Hanlon 33
O'Hanrahan 25
O'Hara 31, 79

O'Hare 33
O'Hart 79
O'Hartly 63
O'Harvy 51
O'Hayden 37
O'Heany 33
O'Heffernan 67
O'Hegarty 49
O'Hehir 25
O'Hennessy 71, 86
O'Henry 83
O'Heron 33
O'Hickey 25
O'Higgins 79
O'Hoey 33
O'Holohan 86
O'Hood 31
O'Horan 57
O'Hussey 55
O'Keally (Kelly) 59
O'Keane 75
O'Keeffe 47
O'Keelaghan 33
O'Keenan 55
O'Kelliher 39
O'Kelly 45, 49, 57, 71
O'Kennedy 81
O'Kernaghan 53
O'Kinnealy 67
O'Kirby 67
O'Langan 33
O'Laverty 83
O'Lavery 31
O'Lavin 77
O'Lawlor 59
O'Lonergan 81
O'Long 39
O'Loughery 79

THINGS IRISH

ANTHONY BLUETT

Things Irish provides the reader with an entertaining and informative view of Ireland, seen through the practices, beliefs and everyday objects that seem to belong specifically to this country. Discarding the usual format of chapters on a variety of themes, the book uses short descriptive passages on anything from whiskey to standing stones, from May Day to hurling, in order to create a distinctive image of Irish life. The reader is free to roam from topic to topic, from passage to passage, discovering a wealth of new and surprising facts and having a number of misguided beliefs put right.

AN INTRODUCTION TO
IRISH HIGH CROSSES

HILARY RICHARDSON & JOHN SCARRY

The Irish high crosses are the most original and interesting of all the monuments which stud the Irish landscape. They are of international importance in early medieval art. For their period there is little to equal them in the sculpture of western Europe as a whole.

This beautiful book gives basic information about the crosses. A general survey is followed by an inventory to accompany the large collection of photographs which illustrate their variety and richness. In this way readers will readily have at their disposal an extensive range of the images created in stone by sculptors working in Ireland over a thousand years ago.

THE COURSE OF IRISH HISTORY

EDITED BY T. W. MOODY AND F. X. MARTIN

A revised and enlarged version of this classic book provides a rapid short survey, with geographical introduction, of the whole course of Ireland's history. Based on a series of television programmes, it is designed to be both popular and authoritative, concise but comprehensive, highly selective but balanced and fair-minded, critical but constructive and sympathetic. A distinctive feature is its wealth of illustrations.

THE GREAT IRISH FAMINE

EDITED BY CATHAL PÓIRTÉIR

This is the most wide-ranging series of essays ever published on the Great Irish Famine and will prove of lasting interest to the general reader. Leading historians, economists, geographers – from Ireland, Britain and the United States – have assembled the most up-to-date research from a wide spectrum of disciplines, including medicine, folklore and literature, to give the fullest account yet of the background and consequences of the Famine.

IRISH CARVED ORNAMENT

H. S. CRAWFORD

This classic book was first published in 1926 by the Royal Society of Antiquaries. Henry Crawford describes in detail the ornamentation of stone monuments, reproducing in the book some 300 illustrations. His photographic 'restorations' of badly weathered stones are unique and this work stands as a testimony to his patient dedication to creating the right natural lighting conditions to display the beauty and clarity of these precious works of art.